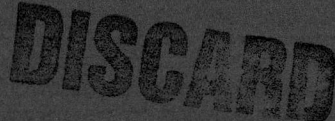

CULTURE IN ACTION
The Orchestra

Liz Miles

Chicago, Illinois

www.heinemannraintree.com
Visit our website to find out more information about Heinemann-Raintree books.

To order:
☏ Phone 888-454-2279
💻 Visit www.heinemannraintree.com to browse our catalog and order online.

©2010 Raintree
an imprint of Capstone Global Library, LLC
Chicago, Illinois

All rights reserved. No part of this publication may be reproduced or transmitted in any form or by any means, electronic or mechanical, including photocopying, recording, taping, or any information storage and retrieval system, without permission in writing from the publisher.

Edited by Louise Galpine, Abby Colich, and Laura J. Hensley
Designed by Kimberly Miracle and Betsy Wernert
Original illustrations © Capstone Global Library Ltd.
Illustrated by kja-artists.com
Picture research by Hannah Taylor
Production by Alison Parsons
Originated by Dot Gradations Ltd.
Printed and Bound in the United States by Corporate Graphics

13 12 11 10 09
10 9 8 7 6 5 4 3 2 1

Library of Congress Cataloging-in-Publication Data

Miles, Liz.
  The orchestra / Liz Miles.
    p. cm. -- (Culture in action)
  Includes bibliographical references and index.
  ISBN 978-1-4109-3394-2 (hc) -- ISBN 978-1-4109-3411-6 (pb)
  1. Orchestra--Juvenile literature. I. Title.
  ML1200.M55 2008
  784.2--dc22
                                    2008053047

Acknowledgments

The author and publishers are grateful to the following for permission to reproduce copyright material: Alamy Images pp. 5 (© Ambient Images Inc.), 11 (© Ruskin Photos), **12 top** (© Lebrecht Music & Arts Library), 26 (© Gari Wyn Williams), **29 top** (© GFC Collection), **29 bottom** (© Ted Foxx); Corbis pp. 6 (The Gallery Collection), 9 (Michael Pole), 17 (Robbie Jack), **24 bottom** (Tim Pannell); Getty Images p. 15 (Steven Harris); © Lebrecht Music & Arts Photo Library p. 28 (Tamsin Lewis); Lebrecht Music & Arts Library pp. 4 & 27 (© C. Christodoulou), **12 bottom** (© Nigel Luckhurst), 14, **24 top** (© Photofest); Photolibrary pp. 16 (Tips Italia/Focus Database), 23 (Visions LLC); Photoshot p. 20 (Imagebrokers/Thomas Frey); Rex Features pp. 18 (Jonathan Player), 21 (Sipa Press), 22 (Everett Collection/CSU Archives); Shutterstock p. 8 (© Thomas Amby); Topfoto p. 10 (ArenaPAL/Dan Porges).

Icon and banner images supplied by Shutterstock: © Alexander Lukin, © ornitopter, © Colorlife, and © David S. Rose.

Cover photograph of an orchestra in a pit at the Opéra Garnier, Paris, France, reproduced with permission of Masterfile/© George Simhoni.

We would like to thank Nancy Harris, Jackie Murphy, Ken Cerniglia, and Colleen Rosati for their invaluable help in the preparation of this book.

Every effort has been made to contact copyright holders of any material reproduced in this book. Any omissions will be rectified in subsequent printings if notice is given to the publisher.

All the Internet addresses (URLs) given in this book were valid at the time of going to press. However, due to the dynamic nature of the Internet, some addresses may have changed, or sites may have changed or ceased to exist since publication. While the author and publisher regret any inconvenience this may cause readers, no responsibility for any such changes can be accepted by either the author or the publisher.

Contents

What Is an Orchestra? 4

A Brief History of Orchestras 6

What Does an Orchestra Include? 8

The Music 14

Famous Orchestral Composers 20

Life in an Orchestra 26

Musicians of the World 28

Glossary 30

Find Out More 31

Index 32

Some words are printed in bold, **like this**. You can find out what they mean by looking in the glossary on page 30.

What Is an Orchestra?

An orchestra is a large group of musicians, often led by a **conductor** (see box below). An orchestra entertains an audience with music. It is fun to play in an orchestra, too.

A full-size **symphony** orchestra usually has around 100 musicians. It has four different sections of musical instruments. Smaller orchestras may have only ten musicians and one section of instruments. An **ensemble** is a small group of musicians, such as a **woodwind** ensemble.

Waving a baton

Most large orchestras have a conductor who leads them. The conductor stands in front of the orchestra, with his or her back to the audience. He or she uses a stick, called a baton, to direct the musicians. The conductor makes sure the musicians keep the beat and play well together.

Conductors such as Marin Alsop work hard with orchestras to get the music to sound right.

The San Diego Symphony Orchestra has been performing concerts for nearly 100 years.

Symphony orchestras

A full-size orchestra that plays **classical music** is called a symphony orchestra, or a **philharmonic** orchestra. Classical music is music written between 1750 and 1820. It is also music that is considered more lasting than pop music. This book focuses on symphony orchestras and the music they play.

Symphony orchestras often perform in big concert halls. For example, the Sydney Symphony Orchestra often performs at the Sydney **Opera** House in Australia. More than 2,600 people can sit together and listen to the orchestra's 110 musicians.

Orchestral roots

The ancient Greeks first used the word *orchestra* more than 2,500 years ago. It was used to describe the area of a theater in front of a stage. In ancient times, performers danced and sang in this space.

5

A Brief History of Orchestras

Ancient times to the Middle Ages (2700 BCE–1450 CE)

around 2686 BCE — The first groups of musicians begin to play together in ancient Egypt about 5,000 years ago. The musicians play pipes, flutes, and drums.

1400 CE — During the Middle Ages (500 CE–1450 CE) in Europe, small groups of musicians entertain people. They play recorders, lutes (instruments similar to guitars), and viols (instruments similar to cellos).

This painting shows musicians from the Middle Ages.

The Renaissance (1450–1600)

late 1500s — The first small orchestras play music in Europe. They play for dances and **operas** (stories told through dancing and singing). They also play for religious events such as church services.

The Baroque period (1600–1750)

mid-1600s — **Composers** begin to write music for specific groups of instruments. **Symphonies** that include more instruments become popular.

The Classical period (1750–1820)

mid-1700s — For the first time, orchestras are no longer just playing **background** music. Large orchestras now need **conductors** to guide them.

The Romantic period (1820–1915)

mid-1800s — Rich music is written with themes such as nature's beauty. The new style of Romantic music mixes many different sounds. It needs more instruments, such as a larger number of **string** instruments. Instruments such as the tuba are added, too.

The Modern period (1915–today)

"Anything goes!" could be the saying for the Modern period. Composers draw from popular music such as **jazz**, rock, and rap. Unusual instruments, such as the banjo, begin to be used in orchestras, too.

Multi-orchestras

Multi-orchestras are concerts in which several groups of musicians play at the same time. They began to appear during the Modern period. Each group of musicians plays in different styles or at different speeds, all at the same time. One Russian composer wrote a symphony that needs nine conductors!

What Does an Orchestra Include?

Traditional orchestras, such as **symphony** orchestras, are usually made up of four sections. They are the **strings**, **woodwind**, **brass**, and **percussion** sections. Each group of players sits in a specific place. The sections with the loudest instruments are percussion and brass, so they are at the back. The quietest instruments are violins, violas, and cellos, in the strings section. They are at the front.

First or second?

In an orchestra, the violins are usually split into two sections. This is because many **composers** have written two separate parts for the violins.

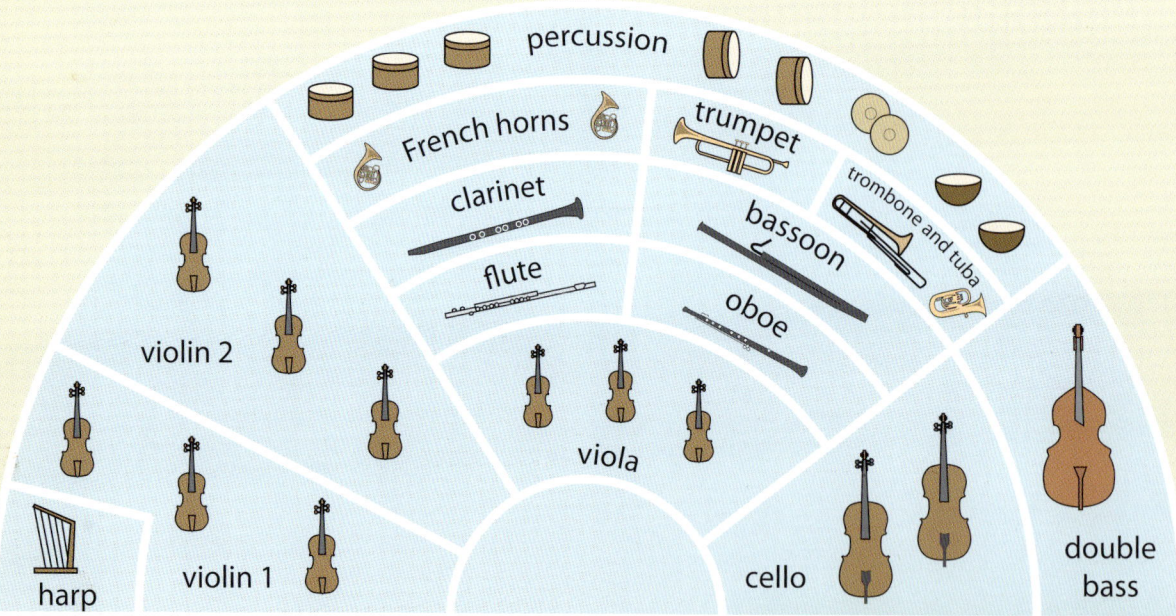

Orchestras sit in a half-circle shape. The seating of musicians is planned so that the sound mixes well.

Strings section

The strings section is the largest part of an orchestra. An orchestra can have a full strings section of 60 instruments! A strings section includes instruments from the violin family. It usually has more violins than any other instrument. It might have 20 or more violins, 8 or more violas and cellos, and 6 double bases. It may have a harp, too. A harp has a large triangular frame, with strings stretched across the triangle. To play a harp, the musician plucks the strings with his or her fingers.

String sounds

String instruments can have many different sounds. When a bow is pulled slowly along a string, string instruments can have a sad sound. When strings are plucked or the bow is pulled quickly, a happy sound can be produced.

String instruments are played by pulling a bow across the strings or by plucking the strings.

Woodwind section

In a full orchestra, the woodwind section has two to four flutes, oboes, clarinets, and bassoons. In the 1700s and 1800s, woodwind instruments were made from wood. Today, they are made from wood, metal, and plastic.

Players blow into woodwind instruments to make sounds. The blown air **vibrates** (moves back and forth quickly) in the tube of the instrument to produce different **notes** (single sounds). When a player covers holes on the instrument, this varies the notes. Generally, the longer and wider the woodwind instrument is, the deeper its sound. Short instruments like the flute have the highest range of high to low sounds in an orchestra. The long, wide bassoon has a deep sound.

Mouthpieces

Many woodwind instruments, such as clarinets and oboes, have thin pieces of material called reeds attached to their mouthpieces. When blown, the reed vibrates against the mouthpiece. As the vibrating air passes through the instrument, it produces sound.

The sound of a flute blends well with many other instruments.

Brass section

The brass section produces some of the boldest sounds in an orchestra. A full orchestra includes two or more trumpets, French horns, trombones, and tubas. Cornets and alto horns may also be used.

All brass instruments are made from coiled tubes of metal. The sound comes from the player's pursed, vibrating lips as he or she blows into a mouthpiece (see box at left). For some brass instruments, the notes from the vibrations can be changed by the player closing or opening valves or keys. They can also be changed by the player changing the tightness of his or her lips.

Like all brass players, these trumpet players have to shape their lips carefully and blow hard to make the right sounds.

Percussion section

Many different percussion instruments are played in orchestras. Percussion instruments create sound when someone strikes or shakes them. They are divided in two groups: **tuned** and untuned. Xylophones and bells are tuned instruments. They make musical notes. Cymbals and tambourines are untuned. They only produce soft or loud sounds. The piano is often classed as a tuned percussion instrument because its strings are hit by tiny hammers. It is also sometimes classed as a string instrument, however, because it has strings.

timpani

Timpani are tuned instruments. A full orchestra has at least two timpani, but it can have as many as ten!

More than just a drum

In an orchestra, a percussionist often plays more than one instrument. The instruments have to be laid out so he or she can easily get from one to another. Percussionists can make booming clashes and bangs. But they also play along with the tune of a song or provide **rhythm** (a regular beat).

Percussionists sometimes have to learn to play strange new instruments for a special piece of music. This man plays a unique instrument called a waterphone. In front of him are a variety of tin cans.

ART ACTIVITY

Painting the orchestra

This activity involves two of the senses: hearing and seeing. By linking music and art, you will create something unique.

Steps to follow:

1. Find a recording of **classical music** that uses every section of the orchestra. You could use Benjamin Britten's "The Young Person's Guide to the Orchestra."

2. Think about how each section of the orchestra sounds: strings, woodwind, brass, and percussion. What is the tone of the instruments? Does the section have a high **pitch** (sound), or is it deep and booming? What is the mood of the instruments—happy or sad? How loud or soft are the instruments?

3. Using paint, brushes, and paper, draw or paint four pictures, one for each section of the orchestra. Your pictures should show how each section of the orchestra makes you feel. You can draw or paint people or animals, or simply use different shapes and colors.

   Add shading to match the volume. Dramatic, loud sounds need deeper shading than soft, quiet sounds. Add happy colors such as orange for music that makes you feel happy. Add sad colors such as black to show a sad mood.

4. Display your artwork for others to see.

Different landscapes show different moods, from soft, hilly landscapes to fiery volcanic mountains.

The Music

All kinds of music are written for orchestras. Usually **composers** write music for the orchestra alone. Sometimes music is written for an orchestra that accompanies a soloist, such as one piano player.

Symphonies

A **symphony** is a musical **composition** (written piece) for an orchestra. Symphonies are divided into sections called **movements**. Symphonies are made up of between one and six movements. Most have four movements. Each movement has a different **tempo** (speed). Most symphonies follow this pattern:

1st movement: Fast
2nd movement: Slowest
3rd movement: Dancelike
4th movement: A lively finale (end).

How to play

Composers write instructions about how their music should be played. Here are some of the words they use:
presto = very fast
allegro = fast and bright, like a march
andante = steadily
adagio = fairly slow, stately
largo = very slow

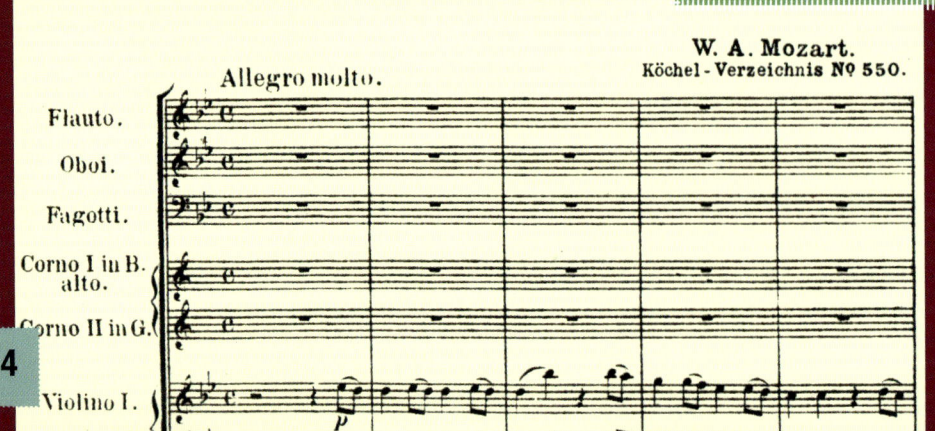

On this sheet music from a symphony by Mozart, you can see the instruction *allegro molto*. This means the music should be played very fast and brightly.

This orchestra is accompanying famous solo singers and a chorus at a concert in China.

Most symphonies have a number in their title, such as Symphony no. 3. But some symphonies have names given by the composer. For example, the German composer Ludwig van Beethoven called his Symphony no. 6 "Recollections of Country Life." Some symphonies get a nickname over time. Austrian composer Joseph Haydn's Symphony no. 94 is called the "Surprise Symphony." It is nicknamed this because it includes a surprisingly loud **chord** (several **notes** played at once).

Some symphonies include small parts for solo players. A **chorus** (group of singers) may also be included in symphonies.

Record breakers

Symphonies can be short or long. The longest symphony is about two hours. The shortest, known as the "Shrunken Symphony," is six minutes. Most symphonies last about an hour.

In the pit

Members of orchestras that play during operas and ballets usually sit in an orchestra pit. This low-level area lies between the stage and the audience. Sometimes it is tucked below the stage as well. The low level keeps the orchestral music from being louder than the voices on stage. Also, the musicians do not block the audience's view of the singers and dancers!

A pit orchestra sits at the base of a stage in a theater.

Orchestras for the stage

Orchestras often accompany dancing, singing, and acting in ballets, **operas**, and musical theater. Orchestral music reflects the action and mood of a story. Orchestras play stage music, too, such as between scene changes during a play.

Orchestras have been used in operas for hundreds of years. An opera tells a story through singing and acting. Opera has been popular since the 1700s. Some operas are funny and some are tragic, so the music ranges in mood.

The size of an opera orchestra ranges, too. For a grand opera, the orchestra can have more than 100 musicians. Grand operas became popular in the 1800s. Large numbers of singers perform in them, so they are exciting to see as well as hear.

Ballet

Orchestras play during ballets to help present a story, mood, and characters. Special instruments can be used for different characters. *The Nutcracker* is a ballet set to orchestral music. It includes a keyboard instrument called a celesta, which sounds similar to chimes. The music also uses children's instruments, including a rattle, cuckoo, toy trumpet, and toy drum. These instruments work with the ballet's fairy-tale theme.

The Sugar Plum Fairy and prince dance in *The Nutcracker* ballet.

Orchestras today

Today's orchestras play music for movies, television shows, and music videos. **Classical music** is often used in movie **soundtracks** (see box below).

Popular bands sometimes use orchestras in their music. Classical orchestras may also play and record popular music by bands such as ABBA and the Beatles.

Movie soundtracks

Sometimes an orchestra is used to record music for a movie soundtrack (the **background** music in a movie). First, the composer receives an early copy of the movie. Next, he or she composes the music for the soundtrack. The orchestra then practices playing the music in front of a large screen on which the movie is shown. Finally, the music is recorded and edited.

Composer John Williams wrote the theme music for the *Star Wars* movies.

MUSIC ACTIVITY

Take up the baton

Try conducting an orchestra using Russian composer Sergei Prokofiev's "Dance of the Knights." Imagine an orchestra sits in front of you. Use one hand to show the beat of the music. Use the other to direct the orchestra.

Steps to follow:

1. Hold a stick (your baton) in your right hand and use it to beat the time. A **time signature** is how many beats there are to a bar (small section) in a piece of music. The time signature for "Dance of the Knights" is 4:4. To beat the 4:4 time, use your baton to draw the shape shown in the picture.

2. Follow the beat of the music and repeat drawing the shape in the air. Move your baton quickly for faster parts of the music and slowly for slower parts.

3. Use your left hand to bring in different parts of the orchestra. You can also raise your left palm for louder playing or lower it when you want the orchestra to play more quietly.

4. Try conducting pieces of music that have different time signatures.

In your own style

Different **conductors** have different styles. Some conductors move in a more controlled way, while others might move around a lot. The U.S. conductor Leonard Bernstein used facial expressions and waved his hands and arms all over the place!

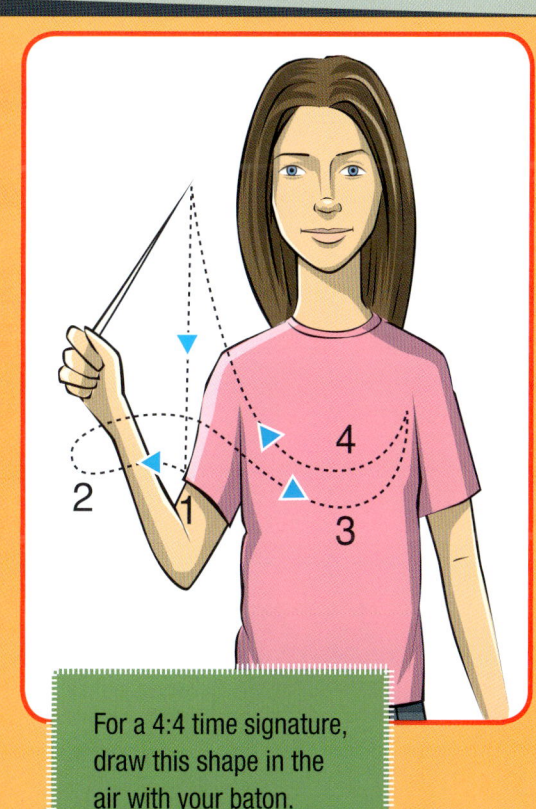

For a 4:4 time signature, draw this shape in the air with your baton.

19

Famous Orchestral Composers

Many **composers**, past and present, have written the music played by the orchestras of today. Here are a few famous names.

George Frideric Handel (1685–1759)

Handel was born in Germany during the Baroque period (see page 6). He wrote music for kings, queens, and churches. Handel composed "Water Music" for King George I of Great Britain. The king wanted to hold a concert on the Thames River, in London, England. An orchestra of 50 musicians played "Water Music" on a boat next to the king's boat.

Some years later, King George II paid Handel to compose "Music for the Royal Fireworks" for a fireworks display in London.

Handel's "Music for the Royal Fireworks" is often played at outdoor concerts. It is accompanied by a dramatic fireworks display.

Wolfgang Amadeus Mozart (1756–1791)

Mozart was born in Austria during the Classical period (see page 7). He was one of the first important composers of **symphonies**. Mozart began composing when he was just four years old. He toured Europe, performing his music. He died at the age of 35, but he wrote a lot of music in his short life. He wrote at least 41 symphonies, 27 piano **concerti** (works written for a solo instrument and an orchestra), and 18 **operas**!

Mozart's music was hard to play. As a result it was not performed as often as the music of other popular musicians. Over time, Mozart's music made musicians work harder. Some people believe that orchestras raised their standards because of Mozart's challenging works.

Mozart wrote his first symphony when he was eight years old!

A winner

Mozart's music for the clarinet made it into a popular instrument. In 2006 his "Clarinet Concerto in A Major" was voted his greatest work by a group of his fans. This happened on the 250th anniversary of Mozart's birth in Austria.

Ludwig van Beethoven (1770–1827)

Beethoven was born in Germany. He was the first composer to use a **chorus** in a symphony (in Symphony no. 9). He was also the first to use trombones, the piccolo, and the double bassoon.

Unlike Mozart, Beethoven let his mood affect his musical **compositions**. His feelings enriched his music. For example, the final **movement** (section) of his Ninth Symphony is so lively that it is often called "Ode to Joy."

Beethoven began to lose his hearing in his twenties. By his mid-thirties he was completely deaf. People are often surprised that "Ode to Joy" was written long after he had become deaf. The depth of feeling in Beethoven's music had a big influence on the next group of composers—the Romantics (see page 7).

Beethoven put his feelings into his compositions.

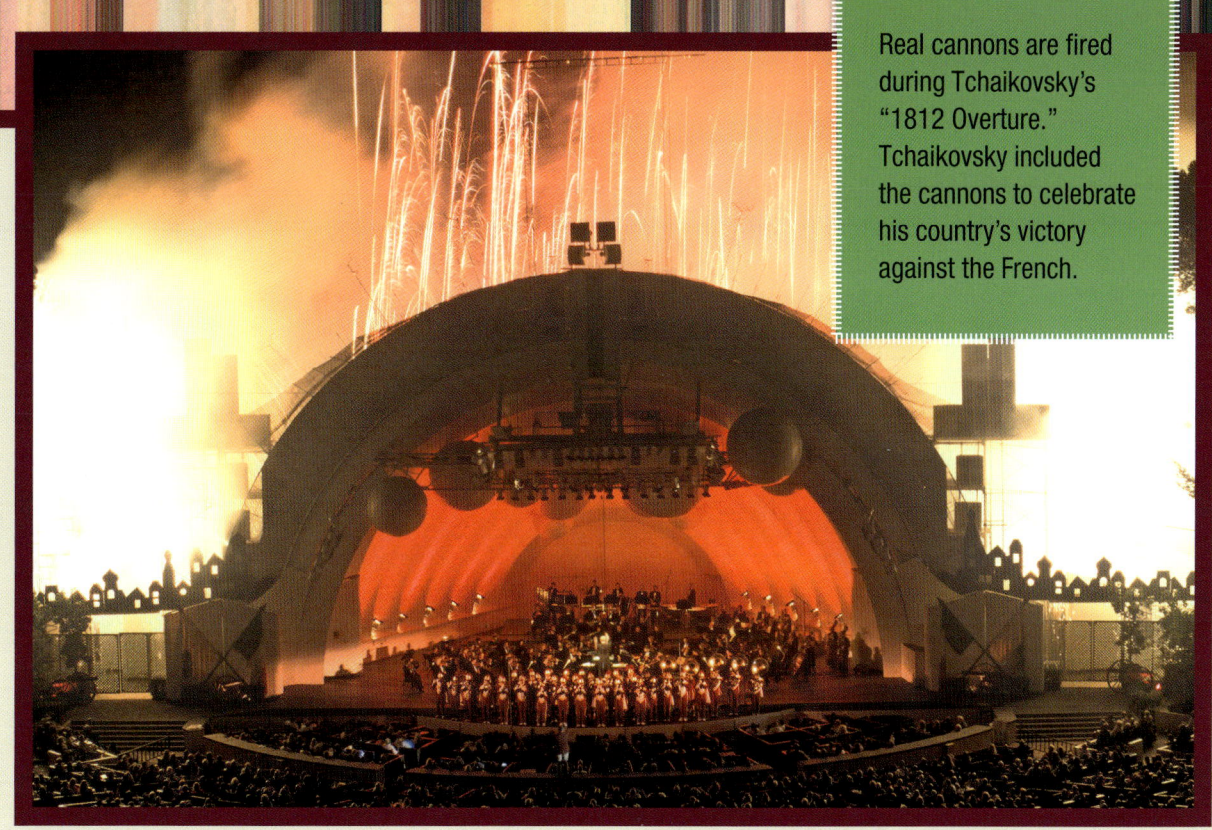

Real cannons are fired during Tchaikovsky's "1812 Overture." Tchaikovsky included the cannons to celebrate his country's victory against the French.

Pyotr Ilich Tchaikovsky (1840–1893)

Tchaikovsky was born in Russia. He was one of several composers during the Romantic period. Like others during this period, he wrote music about how he felt.

Tchaikovsky also wrote nationalistic music that showed his feelings for his own country. His love of Russian **folk music** (music of the common people) also affected the music he composed.

Gustav Mahler (1860–1911)

Composers of the Romantic period started to use more instruments. Before the Austrian composer Mahler, most composers used a very small **percussion** section in the orchestra. Mahler used 20 different percussion instruments in his symphonies. He also wrote the longest symphony. It lasts about two hours. To hear his love for percussion, listen to his Symphony no. 6.

Aaron Copland (1900–1990)

U.S. composer Copland is well known for using cowboy-style music for his cowboy ballets, such as *Billy the Kid*. He was also one of the first to include spoken words in orchestral music.

This shows a scene from Copland's ballet *Billy the Kid*.

Benjamin Britten (1913–1976)

Britten, an Englishman, began composing when he was five years old. He composed a piece of famous music called "The Young Person's Guide to the Orchestra."

Karlheinz Stockhausen (1928–2007)

German composer Stockhausen experimented with all kinds of instruments and electronic music. His "Gruppen for Three Orchestras" uses 109 musicians in three orchestras.

Young composers

Young composers today have many opportunities. The Very Young Composer's Program at the New York **Philharmonic** helps 10-year-old and 11-year-old composers. Kids write down their musical ideas so that the orchestra can play them!

These young people work at a young composers' workshop.

PERFORMANCE ACTIVITY

Accompany an orchestra

Feel what it is like to play an instrument in an orchestra.

Steps to follow:

1. Borrow a percussion instrument or find something to use as a percussion instrument. You could use an overturned bucket and a wooden spoon.

2. Choose a short piece of music, such as Tchaikovsky's "1812 Overture." This is about 15 minutes long.

3. Listen to the music and decide where and how to play your instrument to be a part of the orchestra.

4. Try to play along. See if you can make your instrument add to the changing mood of the piece. For the "1812 Overture," you should begin by playing quietly. Then play along with the louder beats as the music gets bolder. Try to match the beat of the music.

If you can't get a percussion instrument, simply turn a bucket upside down. Play it by hitting the bottom with the handle of a wooden spoon!

Life in an Orchestra

Imagine doing what you love most every day. Many orchestral musicians are doing just that. They love to play their instruments, and they get to make a career out of it. However, it is not easy to achieve this level of success. You have to:

1. Learn to play at least one instrument very well (two is better).
2. Join a local orchestra or your school orchestra.
3. Be prepared to practice a lot and to study hard. Most successful musicians go to college or a music school.

A musician's life

A musician's life is a busy one. Most **professional** musicians practice several hours every day. They take care of their instruments and know how to **tune** them quickly. Tuning an instrument means adjusting it so that it sounds right. A job in an orchestra involves lots of practice, too. Orchestras often travel the world to give concerts.

Instruments—both large and small—must be carried everywhere by their players.

The Royal Albert Hall in London is one of many places where famous orchestras play. There is room for an audience of more than 5,000.

For many musicians, it is a thrill to perform in a concert hall. They love to hear the applause of an audience. Some musicians get nervous before a performance. But they must have steady hands by the time they go on stage.

Orchestral roles

You do not have to be a musician to be in an orchestra. Orchestras need a lot of organizing. People work for orchestras by raising money, organizing tours, and finding the right musicians. These are people who also enjoy music and like to work with musicians.

Musicians of the World

People of all ages, and from different countries, play in orchestras all around the world. There are many different types of instruments around the world, too. In India, for example, the sitar is a popular **string** instrument in orchestras. In South America, the panpipe is a popular **woodwind** instrument.

China

Famous orchestras outside the United States and Europe include the Shanghai Traditional Instruments Orchestra from China. This 80-musician orchestra plays traditional Chinese instruments such as gongs and bamboo flutes. Some musicians play the pipa, a guitarlike instrument with four or five strings. This orchestra tours all over the world.

These children are learning to play traditional Chinese instruments in a music school in Shanghai, China.

Indonesia

Gamelan orchestras are from Indonesia. Their instruments, such as gongs, xylophones, bells, and drums, are hit to make sounds. The musicians play a repeated, intense **rhythm**. This music sounds very different from other styles of music.

Africa

Traditional African orchestras use a variety of instruments to play music composed by Africans. An African instrument called a talking drum is hit with a stick. It also has strings. These are squeezed by the player to change the **pitch**. The noises produced can sound similar to someone talking.

Talking drums are sometimes used to sound out words or messages.

School and youth orchestras

Wherever you live, school orchestras are a great way to gain experience playing in an orchestra. Some young musicians can join a youth orchestra in their community. Musicians have to pass an audition to get into a good youth orchestra.

Young musicians come from all over the world to join the best youth orchestras.

Glossary

background type of music that is usually quiet and not very noticeable

brass type of musical instrument made from coiled tubes of metal, such as a trumpet

chord several notes (single sounds) played at the same time

chorus group of singers

classical music music written between 1750 and 1820, or music that is more lasting than pop music

composer person who writes music

composition written piece of music

concerto (more than one: **concerti**) piece of music for one or more solo instrument and an orchestra

conductor person who leads an orchestra

ensemble small group of musicians

folk music music of the common people of a country or region

jazz type of music that has a strong rhythm or pattern of beats. Jazz musicians often make up the music as they play.

movement separate section of music in a composition such as a symphony

note single sound in music

opera story told through dancing and singing

percussion type of musical instrument that is struck or shaken to make sound, such as drums and tambourines

philharmonic another name for a symphony orchestra. Like symphony orchestras, philharmonic orchestras often play classical music and symphonies.

pitch how high or low a sound is

professional person who is paid for his or her work

rhythm regular beat. In an orchestra, the percussion instruments usually keep the rhythm.

soundtrack background music in a movie

string thread, wire, or nylon that is stretched across some instruments. String instruments have several strings that are plucked or played with a bow.

symphony piece of music written for an orchestra that usually has four movements (sections)

tempo speed

time signature how many beats there are to a bar (small section) in a piece of music

tune way of adjusting instruments so that the notes sound right. It also describes an instrument on which you can play notes and pitches. Chimes are tuned percussion instruments, while a gong is an untuned percussion instrument.

vibrate move back and forth very quickly

woodwind type of instrument that you blow into. Woodwind instruments are made from wood, metal, or plastic.

Find Out More

Books

Koscielniak, Bruce. *The Story of the Incredible Orchestra*. Boston: Houghton Mifflin, 2000.

Levine, Robert. *The Story of the Orchestra: Listen While You Learn About the Instruments, the Music, and the Composers Who Wrote the Music!* New York: Black Dog & Leventhal, 2001.

Masters of Music series. Hockessin, Del.: Mitchell Lane, 2004–2005.

Websites

National Music Museum
www.usd.edu/smm

Dallas Symphony Orchestra Music Room
www.dsokids.com/2001/rooms/musicroom.asp

San Francisco Symphony: SFS Kids
www.sfskids.org/templates/splash.asp

The New York Philharmonic Kidzone
www.nyphilkids.org

Place to visit

National Music Museum
The University of South Dakota
414 East Clark Street
Vermillion, South Dakota 57069

Index

adagio 14
Africa 29
allegro 14
andante 14

background music 7, 18
ballet 16, 17, 24
Baroque period 6
bassoon 10, 22
baton 4, 19
Beethoven, Ludwig van 15, 22
Bernstein, Leonard 19
brass instruments 8, 11
Britten, Benjamin 13, 24

China 15, 28
chorus 15, 22
clarinet 10, 21
classical music 5, 13, 18
Classical period 7
composers 6, 7, 8, 14, 15, 18, 19, 20–24
   young composers 24
concerti 21
conductors 4, 7, 19
Copland, Aaron 24

Egypt, ancient 6
electronic music 24
ensembles 4

flute 6, 10, 28
folk music 23

Handel, George Frideric 20
harp 9
Haydn, Joseph 15

Indonesia 28

jazz 7

largo 14

Mahler, Gustav 23
Middle Ages 6
Modern period 7
mouthpieces 10, 11
movie soundtracks 18
Mozart, Wolfgang Amadeus 14, 21
multi-orchestras 7
musical instruments 6, 7, 8
   around the world 28–29
   brass instruments 11
   children's instruments 17
   percussion instruments 12
   string instruments 7, 9, 12
   tuning 26
   woodwind instruments 4, 10
musicians 26–27
   practicing 26
   professional 26–27
   young musicians 29

nationalistic music 23

operas 6, 16, 21
orchestra pit 16
orchestras
   around the world 28–29
   history of 6–7
   multi-orchestras 7
   origin of the word 5
   school and youth orchestras 29
   sections 8–12, 13
   working in 26–27

percussion instruments 8, 12, 23, 25
philharmonic orchestras *see* symphony orchestras

piano 12
piccolo 10, 22
playing in an orchestra 25
pop music 18
presto 14
Prokofiev, Sergei 19

rap 7
Renaissance 6
rhythm 12, 28
rock 7
Romantic period 7, 22, 23

school and youth orchestras 29
seating 8
soloists 14, 15
stage music 16
Stockhausen, Karlheinz 24
string instruments 7, 8, 9, 12, 28
symphonies 6, 14–15, 21, 22
   duration 15, 23
   movements 14
   names 15
symphony orchestras 4, 5, 8

Tchaikovsky, Pyotr Ilich 23
tempo 14
time signature 19
timpani 12
trombone 11, 22
trumpet 11

violin 8, 9

Williams, John 18
woodwind instruments 4, 8, 10